Scimitar

Scimitar

by
D. Gibbings
and
J. A. Gorman

Foreward by Capt. J. Flindell, RN

Drawings by Mike Keep

Society of Friends of the Fleet Air Arm Museum
Monograph No. 3
Series Editor David Gibbings

Photoset in 10/11 Times Roman
Text paper supplied by Howard Smith Papers, Bristol
Bound by J. W. Braithwaite & Sons Ltd, Wolverhampton
Printed in Great Britain by Picton Print
Citadel Works, Bath Road, Chippenham, Wiltshire

'Therefore came I to smite the smiter with the…'

Scimitar

Byron

Cover photo: Scimitar makes a pass at near sonic speed at Farnborough.

FOREWORD

Browsing through my log book I found an entry dated 5th October 1962 which recalled a Hunter sortie during which I did some air to air cine of a Scimitar flown by Simon Creasy and carrying a Bullpup to Benbecula range for a live firing.

The trip was uneventful but the impact of flying close to the large and potent airframe was considerable.

The Scimitar's predecessor was the dainty Sea Hawk, everyone's favourite, an elegant aeroplane whose single engine gave a friendly whistle in the air. The Scimitar was an attractive plane, but its sheer bulk prevented its ever being elegant, and the roar of its twin Avons was far from friendly. Here was a fighter built to mean business.

Although the Scimitar design was rather old by the time the aircraft entered service, its time in the FAA was well spent. Air and ground crew learned all about the problems of operating heavy sophisticated machines from carrier decks, and were well prepared for the next generation of large naval jets.

The Scimitar never saw action, and is in danger of being one of the 'forgotten' aircraft. I hope that this monograph will prevent that happening, and that you will enjoy reading it.

Captain J. Flindell, RN

An evocative scene on ARK ROYAL. Scimitar XD241/150 of 803 Squadron is prepared for first detail.

R. Reardon

DEVELOPMENT

The Scimitar was the last of a long line of Supermarine fighters which can be traced in a unbroken line back to the 1930s, to no less than the Spitfire.

The Spitfire was Supermarine's first fighter design to win official favour. Navalised versions, the Seafires, were the company's first designs to be produced for the Fleet Air Arm. Final development of the Spitfire/Seafire line led to the development of a new laminar flow wing, producing the Spiteful/Seafang series, built as prototypes only. With the advent of the jet engine Supermarine married the Seafang wing to a new fuselage housing a Rolls Royce Nene engine and produced the Attacker, the first jet fighter to equip a frontline naval squadron. A swept wing version of the Attacker was developed as the Swift, one prototype of which became the first swept wing aircraft to operate from a carrier. The Swift series also saw the incorporation of a nosewheel undercarriage and Rolls Royce Avon engines.

War time experience had shown the problems inherent in carrier operation of high performance fighters, in particular the aerodynamically clean Seafire had suffered enormously from its tendency to float on the approach and landing accidents were commonplace. Jet-engined aircraft promised to be even worse, with its introduction the all up weight of land based fighters increased sharply, transonic aerofoils led to higher landing speeds. If shipborne fighters were to be viable it was essential they kept pace with developments, the Admiralty carried out trials of belly landing a Sea Vampire on a flexible deck. An undercarriageless aeroplane would have a higher performance from its reduced weight, it would be launched from a special catapult, and landing on a flexible deck would reduce landing accidents. The Scimitar evolved directly from Supermarine's initial work towards an undercarriageless carrier fighter.

The aircraft, designated the Type 505, was designed with unswept wings. Swept-back wings were considered, but were rejected because of the added complexities. A butterfly tail was chosen, mounted above the jet pipes, in line with the contemporary concern over the high speed characteristics of the conventional tail units. To establish the flight patterns of the type a rigid tricycle undercarriage was fitted and the cockpit layout was very similar to the Attacker. However in 1947 the Admiralty abandoned the idea of undercarriageless aircraft and Supermarine modified the Type 505 with a retractable nosewheel undercarriage and re-designated it the Type 508.

1

The Attacker F.Mk.1. The Royal Navy's first jet fighter represented the link from seafire and utilised the laminar flow wing originally designed for Spiteful.

Supermarine were acquiring swept wing experience with the Swift, and it was becoming obvious that the Type 508 would benefit from the swept wings. Design work began on the swept Type 508, the Supermarine Type 525. In the meantime, the first of the Type 508 prototypes, VX129, was completed and made its first flight on the 31 August 1951 from the Aircraft and Armament Experimental Establishment at Boscombe Down, piloted by Mike Lithgow. Shipboard trials followed aboard EAGLE in May 1952.

Incorporation of the swept wing in the Type 525 necessitated a number of changes from the Type 508, most noticeably the adoption of a conventional tail unit in place of the original butterfly empennage. The first flight of the Type 525, took place from Boscombe Down on 27 April 1954 and later that year VX138, took part in the Society of British Aircraft Constructors show at Farnborough. In July 1955 VX138 crashed into the ground south of Boscombe Down, killing the pilot, Lt. Cdr. Rickell.

The 1950's heralded a period of continuous innovation in aircraft carrier design, driven by the demands arising from increases in weight and landing speeds the angled deck. The steam catapult and mirror approach deck landing (MADL) were all introduced during this exciting phase keeping pace with the advances in airframe and engine technology.

Supermarine had been investigating the aerodynamic effects of boundary layer control. Correct utilisation of surplus high pressure air from jet engine compressors could control the break up of smooth air flow over the flaps in the landing regime. 'Flap blow' or 'supercirculation' was schemed into a further development of the Type 525, the Type 544. The practical result was a substantial reduction in stalling at approach speeds, and improved low speed controllability. The new technique was critical in turning the heavy twin-Avon Scimitar into a respectable deck-landing aeroplane. The first Type 544, WT854, built to specification N113D made its first flight from Boscombe Down on 19 January 1956, the pilot again being Mike Lithgow. The second prototype, WT859, was the first to incorporate the flap blow system, as did the third aircraft, WW134, which was used for the first deck-landing trials.

On 5 April 1956 the first deck landing was made on HMS ARK ROYAL. This was the first time that an aircraft of over 30000 lb had landed on a British carrier. Later that month a test pilot took off with the parking brake on but made a safe circuit and recovery, proving the power of the Rolls Royce Avon engines.

Blown flaps had now become an important aspect of the Scimitar's low speed handling characteristics. On completion of trials the Government ordered 100 aircraft to specification N113P1 and the first production Scimitar, XD212, made its first flight on 11 January 1957.

P. Glazier

The Supermarine 508, which led the way to the Scimitar, here seen engaged in flight deck trials on board EAGLE in May 1952.

Supermarine Type 525 (VX138) at Farnborough.

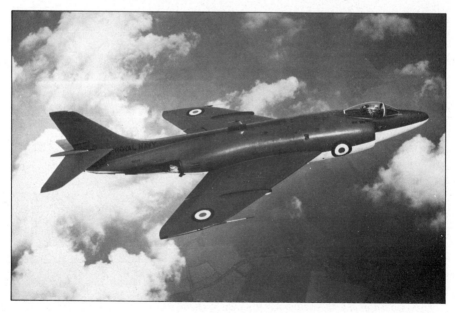

First production Scimitar XD212, which first flew on 11 January 1957.

CONSTRUCTION

The Scimitar marked the end of aircraft design and manufacture by the Supermarine division of Vickers Armstrong (Aircraft).

The all-metal fuselage was of oval section except for the front and rear portions, and was built up of frames, longerons, intercostals and light alloy plating. The front section accommodated the pilot in a pressurized cockpit with an electrically operated jettisonable sliding hood and an ejection seat. Forward of the pressurized region the fuselage nose could be folded back.

The mainplanes were of all-metal construction with forward main and aft spars and were swept back 45 degrees, Hydraulically-powered mainplane folding was provided. Trailing edge flaps were fitted to the inner mainplanes and leading edge flaps were fitted to both inner and outer mainplanes.

Hydraulically operated air brakes were provided and comprised six small flaps (mounted three each side of the fuselage) installed, just forward of the jet pipe outlets. Aft of these outlets the fuselage became circular and merged into the empennage.

The empennage or trail plane structure was built up to carry the swept back fin, the tailplane and its hydraulic actuator, the tailskid, arrestor hook and holdback gear used in catapult launches. The tail skid and deck hook were retractable, with fixed farings and doors to complete the contour. After the butterfly tail of the Type 508 had been rejected the Type 525 was fitted with an all-flying tailplane with ten degrees dihedral. To reduce the 'pitch up' effect experienced at high speeds and altitudes, production Scimitars were fitted with tailplanes of ten degrees anhedral.

Early operational experience with the Scimitar also identified a structural problem in the tail area, with fatigue cracking caused by engine noise. The tail area was modified with steel ribs and thicker alloy panels with bonded foam backing, and the fatigue life was raised to acceptable levels.

Flying controls were hydraulically operated and were controlled by a conventional control column and rudder bar. The tailplane and ailerons were powered by a dual hydraulic system, the first instance in a British naval aircraft. The rudder, which was powered by one system only, reverted to manual control in the event of hydraulic failure. Hydraulic feel simulation was provided for the tailplane and rudder controls and spring feel for the ailerons. Electrically controlled actuators for trimming were fitted into each control run and the tailplane was interconnected with the trailing edge flaps.

Fuel was carried in five bag tanks in the fuselage and four integral tanks in the mainplanes. Provision was made for the carriage of four pylon-mounted drop tanks beneath the mainplanes. The fuel system was pressurised and a complex and often troublesome balance system regulated the supply from individual internal tanks. A fuel proportioner controlled the supply for fuel from the jettisonable drop tanks. Two recuperators maintained a supply of fuel to the engines for a limited period when the aircraft was subjected to negative g conditions.

The electrical system was a 28V DC single pole earth return system powered by two engine driven 28V 6KW wide speed generators. AC power for instruments, radio etc was supplied by two 115V 3-phase inverters which employed an automatic changeover circuit giving standby facilities. Radio services included VHF communication and homing system, telebriefing, radio altimeter and navigational and operational aids.

At near sonic speed, a Scimitar makes a pass wearing its own little rain-cloud at Farnborough.

Cyril Peckham F.R.P.S.

Two aircraft of 700X Squadron flying from RNAS Ford sometime in 1957.

THE SCIMITAR ENTERS SERVICE

When the Scimitar entered service in 1958 it was the largest, heaviest, noisiest and most powerful fighter the Fleet Air Arm had acquired up to that time. The Naval fighter pilots had thus far only experienced the Sea Hawk and Sea Vampire, with 5/6000 lb of thrust and 15000 lb all up weight. The 30,000 lb Scimitar with 20,000 lb of thrust from two Rolls Royce Avons forced a quantum jump in pilot techniques. The complexity of the aircraft's systems also brought new problems for the Fleet Air Arm's engineers and maintainers. If nothing else, the Scimitar's introduction brought an increased demand for drip trays and dustbins. The abiding memory for most ex-Scimitar personnel is of an aircraft that leaked fuel from every seam imaginable.

Until the formation of 700X flight it was normal naval practice for service trials of fighter types to be split into three catagories, each evaluated by different units. In April 1955 the Directorate of Air Warfare decided that one unit should carry out all three trials, Flight Trials, Tactical Trials and Technical Evaluation for the Scimitar.

On 27 August 1957 700X flight was formed at HMS PEREGRINE, Royal Naval Air Station Ford, under the command of Commander T.G. Innes, AFC. The unit was made up of 8 pilots, 3 engineering officers, 46 CPO's and PO's and 72 junior ratings.

The unit was equipped with 7 aircraft and the objects of the Flight were:

1. To prove the aircraft in its various roles.

2. To evaluate the maintainability of the aircraft as a whole and eliminate as many causes of trouble as possible.

3. To distribute the information gained so that appropriate action could be taken.

7

The primary object was to ensure that the Scimitar entered front line squadrons capable of immediately performing its chosen role and sustaining the role over the longest possible period. Resident with X Flight were an additional pilot and two engineers who were responsible for the development of the Scimitar simulators and cockpit procedure trainers.

After nine months trials with the flight, a period of hard and sometimes frustrating work, the Scimitar was taken into service with the Royal Navy. During the nine months the flight achieved a total of 982 sorties in 935 flying hours. Out of all this the Scimitar had emerged proven and ready for introduction to the front line.

Thus the FAA's first swept wing transonic aircraft, with power unprecedented in the history of the Royal Navy, was ready to support the Fleet. The Commanding Officer of 700X Flight did not live to see the Scimitar enter front line service. Commander Innes was killed in a car crash on 20 March 1958 and his place was taken by Commander J.D. Russell.

700X flight disbanded on 29 May 1958. All the pilots and a large majority of the ground crews were destined to join the first front line Scimitar squadron, 803.

Arrester gear trials at RAE Bedford.

700X Squadron Scimitar (XD221) embarked for trials.

736 SQUADRON

736 Squadron formed at Lossiemouth on 11 May 1959 with the Scimitar, and continued in second line service until July 1965. The primary task of 736 Squadron was to train a pilot in the many tasks that would be demanded of him when he joined a front line Scimitar Squadron. These included photo-reconnaissance, Sidewinder interception, ground attack with guns, bombs, rockets or Bullpup missiles, low level strike navigation and army cooperation. Each student spent 65 flying hours on type before joining an operational unit.

The Squadron was disbanded at Lossiemouth in March 1965 and its remaining Scimitars were transfered to 764B Squadron which was temporarily formed on the same station to provide Scimitar conversions for Airwork pilots.

Scimitar XD227 of 736 Squadron in the tanker role.

764 B SQUADRON

Motto: Experientia expertus (Tested by trial)

764 Squadrons' association with the Scimitar was brief. The Squadron itself which was formed early in World War 2, has during numerous reformation maintained a distinguished record in the important tasks of trials and operational training, operating a wide range of types.

In Febuary 1959 the Squadron briefly operated Scimitars to supplement its Hunters to service its role as an Air Weapons training flight and also a Commanding Officers and Senior Pilots Course

The Squadron was again reformed in March 1965 to operate a conversion unit with the expressed purpose of training Airwork pilots with their conversion to type on Scimitars in their task as a Fleet Requirements Unit.

Although maybe a less glamourous undertaking than that of an operational front line Squadron. 764's contribution must be recognised as typical of much of the Fleet Air Arms supporting activity without which the service would be weaker.

Scimitar fires its Bullpup missile.

11

800 Squadron practising for the Paris Air Show in 1961.

800 SQUADRON

Motto: Nunguam non paratus (Never unprepared)

    800 Squadron recommissioned on 1 July 1958 at RNAS Lossiemouth under the command of Lt. Cdr. D.P. Norman RN. The squadron was equipped with 8 Scimitars, a considerable contrast to the dainty Seahawks which 800 had previously used. Despite such names as 'Dragmasters' the pilots soon formed an attachment to these fast aircraft with a feeling of excessive power. 800 embarked in ARK ROYAL alongside 807 in 1960 and served in her in 1960/61 and 1962/63, finally flying off on New Year's Eve 1963 for RNAS Lossiemouth.

    In 1961 800 Squadron took part in both the Paris Air Show and at Farnborough. With their red tails they became known as the 'Red Blades.' (It had been traditional since before the war for 800 Squadron to wear red on its aircraft.) In May 1963 the 14 aircraft of the squadron joined ARK ROYAL off Majorca in one single flight from Lossiemouth. On 26 February 1964 the squadron disbanded to re-equip with the Blackburn Buccaneer S.Mk 1.

800B SQUADRON

The Squadron was formed in 1964 under Lt. R. Dimmock RN following a problem which arose with the Buccaneer S1. Early operational flying disclosed that the Buccaneer could not be launched at maximum all up weight due to a combined short fall of Gyron Junior engine and carrier catapult power. A small number of Scimitars were fitted with 3,200 gallon underwing drop tanks and a flight refuelling Mark 20 'Buddy' pack, and put to use as tankers. The Scimitars were launched before the Buccaneers, the latter carrying full weapons and minimum fuel loads. The Buccaneer then hooked up to the tanker Scimitar and took on its full fuel load. 800B was embarked in EAGLE between 1964/66 until the more powerful Buccaneer S2 came into service, and the tanker requirement ended.

The distinctive Symbol of an overflowing tankard on the tail followed adoption of the Squadron by Whitbread Breweries and led to the squadron being known as the 'Foaming Tankards'.

As well as providing tanker support for Buccaneers 800B also refuelled Sea Vixens of 899 Squadron and other Services Aircraft including RAF Javelins in the Far East.

Although configured as tankers the Scimitars were nevertheless prepared for use for ground attack during the Indonesian campaign, using their front firing guns.

Scimitar XD268 of 800B Squadron equipped with Mk20 refuelling pod, awaits the launch aboard EAGLE.

13

803 SQUADRON

Motto: Cave punctum (Beware of the sting)

Commander J.D. Russell RN commissioned the first front line squadron, 803, at HMS FULMAR, RNAS Lossiemouth on June 3 1958, equipped with 8 aircraft originally, increased to 12 in 1960.

Before embarking in HMS VICTORIOUS the squadron worked up at Lossiemouth, culminating in its participation in the SBAC Show at Farnborough. Tragically, on Embarkation Day, Commander Russell was killed. As he landed on the ship the arrester wire snapped and his aircraft toppled over the side. Although

Scimitars of 803 Squadron, (XD322/020, XD324/033), operating from ARK ROYAL in 1965.

14

the rescue helicopter was soon over the crash the aircraft sank, taking the pilot with it.

The tragic accident was all the more distressing in that it occurred within full view of newsreel cine cameras. It brought home dramatically the hazards involved in operating modern fighters at sea and, as in the way of such things, led to a review of escape procedures and training. There can be no doubt that this accident was one of the convincing factors which led to the introduction of the underwater escape training which all R.N. fixed wing and helicopter crews now undergo. All naval aviators agree it is one of the more valuable training procedures. Perhaps this is a memorial to a fine aviator.

803 Squadron operated successfully from HMS VICTORIOUS, HERMES and finally ARK ROYAL. As well as being the first, 803 was also the last squadron to operate the Scimitar, finally relinquishing its aircraft in 1966 after returning from the Beira Patrol, with ARK ROYAL.

The Squadron disbanded on 1 October 1966 after 8 years and 5 months in commission.

Prepared for launch from ARK ROYAL, an 803 squadron Scimitar (XD323/157) with the flight refuelling pack clearly visible.

804 SQUADRON

Motto: Swift to kill

804 Squadron recommissioned at Lossiemouth on 1 March 1960, equipped with 6 Supermarine Scimitars under the command of Lt. Cdr. T. Binney RN. After a four month work up period the squadron embarked in HERMES. Except for two periods ashore at Lossiemouth, the squadron operated from HERMES until the unit disbanded in September 1961. The squadron took part in both the Farnborough and Paris Air Shows in 1961, operating from the deck of HERMES, a most unusual way of participating in these major events.

Two Scimitars of 804 squadron, (XD326/163, XD325/165), operating from HERMES in July 1960.

16

Part of the spectacular climax to 807 Squadron's display at Farnborough in 1952. A single aircraft (XD244/191) lands between two taxiing aircraft (XD267/193 and XD248/165).

807 SQUADRON.

Motto: Quoquo versus fenturi (Ready to strike in all directions)

807 Squadron recommissioned on 1 October under the command of Lt Cdr Keith Leppard RN, the ceremony taking place at HMS FULMAR. The Squadron began a hectic work-up period immediately and participated in a major exercise only 15 days after commissioning. 807 remained at Lossiemouth throughout 1959, working up and taking part in exercises and trials. In September the squadron thrilled thousands of spectators at Farnborough with an immaculate display of formation aerobatics.

The 1959 SBAC show at Farnborough was dominated by the spectacular flying skills of the Fleet Air Arm and in particular 807 Squadrons Scimitars commanded by Lt Cdr Keith Leppard RN. The Naval aviators began their swashbuckling display with a six stream take off to form a four aircraft aerobatic team and two soloists. One of the two singletons performed a target banner pick up using an extension to the deck hook, the other carried out a simulated LABS attack.

Meanwhile the four aircraft formation returned for a transonic pass at 700 mph followed by a short aerobatic display. Included in this sequence was what the Naval commentator described as an 'original manoeuvre', a fast pass in open box formation with a rapid individual roll by each Scimitar. The 'Twinkle Roll' was born. The most daring feat was yet to come. The two singletons touched down from the left immediately folding their wings whilst one aircraft from the box of four detached and approached from the right, landing head on between them. A stirring display indeed.

On 10 November 1959 Lt.N.Grier-Rees carried out a successful ejection from a Scimitar after his flying controls locked.

The squadron finally embarked in HMS ARK ROYAL on 3 March 1960 where it remained for the next year, taking part in major exercises and carrying out cold weather trials in the Artic Circle.

In March 1961 807 said goodbye to HMS ARK ROYAL and embarked in April in HMS CENTAUR. It was soon obvious that CENTAUR was not suitable for Scimitar operations. The ship was too slow and too small to allow the aircraft to be operated to their limits. The carrier could not provide the additional wind over the deck needed to launch in hot climates with little natural wind.

Before leaving for the Far East in October 1961 the aircraft were modified to carry Sidewinder and Bullpup missiles, and also with a flight refuelling capability. On 21 October Lt. P.M. Hessey fired the first successful live Sidewinder when he destroyed a Meteor target aircraft over Aberporth Ranges. After 7 months in the Middle and the Far East 807 Squadron disbanded on CENTAUR in Portsmouth on 17 May 1962.

Sortie completed and the wire taken. XD270/191 of 807 Squadron landing on CENTAUR.

FLEET REQUIREMENTS UNIT

As the Scimitar's fighter role was adopted by the Sea Vixen and its strike role by the Buccaneer, the Scimitar was relegated to second line service. Several aircraft passed to the Fleet Requirements Unit. FRU provided aircraft for Fleet Radar Calibration and Gunnery exercises and was a contract organisation, operated by Airwork Ltd., flying from Hurn, Bournemouth. The Scimitar was replaced in FRU duties in 1969/70 by the Hawker Hunter.

ARMAMENT

Originally designed as a single seat interceptor armed with four 30 mm Aden guns, the Scimitar later carried a variety of stores as its operational role changed to that of low level strike.

Four underwing pylons could carry either drop tanks or 500 lbs or 1000 lbs bombs, the latter accompanied by incorporation of a LABS (Low Altitude Bombing Sortie) delivery system. The Scimitar was also modified to carry Sidewinder air-to-air missiles and later Bullpup missiles. Rocket projectiles of either 2″ or 3″ could be carried, and the Scimitar also predated its strike replacement the Buccaneer in having a nuclear capability.

A salvo of eight rocket projectiles fired by a 807 squadron Scimitar (XD248/195). The RP's could be fired in any combination from single to twenty four in salvo.

An 803 Squadron Scimitar (XD241/150) with a single Sidewinder, here taking the wire on ARK ROYAL.

EVALUTION OF THE SCIMITAR

'Jeez! Only the Limeys could put two Avons in an airplane and keep it subsonic'.

The story is apocryphal, and the American airman reputed to have made this statement probably imaginary, but the statement is true. It could equally be applied to the Scimitar, and its interceptor replacement the Sea Vixen.

The Scimitar was transonic in a shallow dive, but its long development to service period meant that its design philosophy was overtaken in the meantime. Although it was stable and controllable in the low-level strike role, its outdated wing design meant that its manoeuverability above 30,000 feet was limited, a poor feature for an interceptor of the 1960s. The Scimitar was regarded as sophisticated at its introduction but systems development meant that pilot workload in the strike role would become unacceptably high. It was inevitable that this role should be adopted by the two seat Buccaneer.

It is unfair to dismiss the Scimitar as a failure. If nothing else it provided the Fleet Air Arm with operational experience of a heavy, complex aeroplane of significantly higher performance than the lightweight jets which had preceded it. As the first example of the second generation of Naval jet fighters, Supermarine could reasonably have expected that the Admiralty would issue contracts to update the Scimitar. A new wing could have created a supersonic interceptor, or a two seat version could have been an effective strike aircraft, capable of accepting systems modernisation and proliferation. The two seat Scimitar, Type 556, to Specification NA/38, was designed as an all weather fighter, but it was cancelled at the mock up stage in 1955 in favour of the Sea Vixen.

Only 76 production Scimitars were ever built and this promising design never approached the fame of its ancestor, the Seafire. It did however serve the Fleet Air Arm well and the lessons learnt from operating the Scimitar, prepared the way for a service which would have to operate Phantoms and Buccaneers from ships barely large enough and which would leave no room for error.

An 807 Squadron Scimitar (XD 248/195) picks up a Dart target during the 1959 SBAC display at Farnborough.

THE DART TARGET

With the advent of modern, high speed, high altitude aircraft, it became obvious that the 'banner' target, towed at 200 knots was most inadequate. The speed and altitude restrictions on the tow vehicle towing a banner, made air to air firing more a matter of missing the target with the aircraft, than of hitting it with the bullets.

In order to satisfy the demands of a high altitude, high speed aerial target, the design needed a shape which was sturdy enough to withstand extreme altitudes and air-speeds, yet possessed a very low drag factor so that these altitudes and air-speeds would be obtainable by the towing aircraft.

The best shape developed was a triangular, four finned, cruciform target with a faired radar reflector at its end. The target was normally constructed of 3/8th inch plywood bolted to an angle iron frame.

The normal methods of launching targets proved unsatisfactory in the case of the dart. The snatch technique, which was a variation of a method used for ground launching gliders, was devised for this type of target. The major items of equipment required were a nylon tow line of 2,000 feet length, two twelve feet poles twenty feet apart, used for raising and spreading the tow line pick-up loop, two twenty five feet poles one hundred and fifty feet apart, to enable the height to be judged and a twelve foot towing hook which was attached to the aircraft by an adaptor mounted on the arrester hook.

The tow line was laid full length on the ground. The down-range end attached to the target, which was restrained only from moving in the direction of the pick-up poles. The up-range end of the tow line terminated in a loop that stretched between the tops of the pick-up poles. The towing aircraft was flown over the pick-up standards towards the target, at an altitude which would allow its towing hook to engage the tow line loop. After a successful engagement, the aircraft climbed steadily up, over and beyond the target. As the tow line lifted from the ground and the point of separation of the line from the ground approached the target, the airload against the tow line shaped it into a modified catenary curve. A strong lift was thus developed by the tow line, which raised the target directly into the air without dragging it. Because of the stretching of the nylon tow cable and the cushioning effect of the tow line catenary, the inertial forces on the target remained low. Thus the target was launched without the attendant dangers of drag and air launching. Since almost all of the shock load was absorbed by the tow line during launch, little yaw was felt in the tow aircraft as the target became airborne.

Because of the Scimitar's high rate of climb and high top speed, it was an ideal aircraft with which to tow the dart. Scimitars towed dart targets in excess of Mach 1 at heights of over 40,000 feet. Modifications included near miss recorders, which were necessary owing to the target's relatively small size.

With the target hook extended and flaps down a Scimitar snatches a target from the carrier deck.

SCIMITAR IN THE FLEET AIR ARM MUSEUM

SUPERMARINE SCIMITAR F.Mk.1 XD317 '112/R'

XD317 was delivered to the Aircraft Holding Unit at Lossiemouth on November 11th 1959. It entered service on February 23rd 1960 with No. 807 Squadron, as '197/R', until March 1961 when it was recoded '197/C'. It returned to the AHU on June 23rd 1961 and was delivered to the Royal Naval Aircraft Yard at Fleetlands on October 20th 1961. It was on strength at the AHU at Tengah, Singapore, from November 3rd 1961 and had joined No. 807 Squadron again on February 12th 1962, this time as '195/C'. It was back at Lossiemouth on June 24th 1962, and at Fleetlands on May 16th ready for issue to No. 736 Squadron on November 28th 1962. On January 14th 1963, it joined No. 800 Squadron as '112/R' – the markings it wears today. It returned to Fleetlands on February 27th 1964 and from there to Lee on November 22nd 1965. Its role now changed to research and it joined the Royal Aircraft Establishment at Thurleigh from January 6th 1966, at Farnborough from March 10th 1966 and back at Thurleigh from April 1st 1966. After this it was flown to the Naval Aircraft Servicing Unit at Brawdy on July 27th ready for issue to the Fleet Requirements Unit. This happened on November 2nd 1966 when it was delivered to Hurn, becoming '033', recoded '833' by 1969. It returned to the RAE and Farnborough on August 4th and was delivered by road to the Museum in September 1969 at the end of its flying life.

THE PICTURE OF SCIMITAR

A fine study of 807 Squadron Scimitars in an impeccable box formation loop.

The first prototype Supermarine N113, WT854, carrying out flight deck trials on ARK ROYAL, July 1956. The prototype Sea Vixen is parked athwartships.

WT854 on the deck of ARK ROYAL.

Flight Deck scene aboard HERMES in July 1962. The Scimitar (XD241/150) belongs to 803 Squadron and the Gannet AEW 3 to 849 B Flight.

Airborne and dropping the strop XD331/145 launching from VICTORIOUS.

Arctic trials with ARK ROYAL. Carried out by 807 Squadron. February 1961. (XD243/190).

One on the catapult, with two following up. The arctic trials in full swing.

One of the most dangerous places in the world, catapult stations, here on the foredeck of VICTORIOUS.

A busy squadron scene as 803 Squadron Scimitars (XD243/147, XD246/153) are ranged on the foredeck of VICTORIOUS.

The Royal Navy display for Farnborough 1962 included 736 Squadron Scimitars pictured here climbing into the loop.

R. Reardon

Scimitars of 803 Squadron in the process of being ranged on the foredeck of ARK ROYAL.

Bob Cunningham

An 803 Squadron aircraft, XD230/145 at point of launch on the port catapult of VICTORIOUS.

Two studies of 800 B Squadron in the act of refuelling. As can be seen with the RAF Javelin, they would serve just about anybody.

31

Not a very forgiving profession, 803 Squadron Scimitar XD269 going over the side on VICTORIOUS following a brake failure, 10 July 1961.

'Just when you thought it was safe...'
Scimitar XD239 of 800 squadron in Aden Harbour, May 1963.

Clear nose, cockpit and intake detail in this picture with refuelling probe prominent.

Naval aviation summed up in a single picture. A fine study of a Scimitar about to take the wire.

INDIVIDUAL AIRCRAFT

* Prototype and Development aircraft.

VX138   Prototype Supermarine Type 525, Crashed Boscombe Down July 1955.
WT854   Prototype Supermarine Type 544. First flight, Boscombe Down
        19th January 1956 flown by Mike Lithgow.
WT859   Second prototype.
WW134   Third prototype used for deck landing trials.

The Admiralty originally ordered 100 aircraft to specification N113P, but only 76 machines were built.

Serials
    XD212 to 250.   XD264 to 282.   XD316 to 333.   Cancelled batch
    XD334 to 357.

XD212   Crashed on ATC exercise 20/9/61. Ex 736 Sqn.
XD213   Crashed near East Chaldon 20/9/63 Ex 803 Sqn.
XD214   Nosewheel collapsed at Yeovilton 28/5/69. Scrapped. Ex FRU.
XD215   Burnt at School of Aircraft Handling Culdrose 1972. Ex 764 Sqn.
XD216   Crashed in sea off West Wittering 16/7/67. Ex E.T.P.S.
XD217   Scrapped at RNAS Brawdy in 1970. Ex 736 Sqn.
XD218   Vickers trials aircraft. Scrapped at Royal Navy Air Yard Fleetlands
        1967.
XD219   Ran off runway at Farnborough during brake trials. Wrecked.
XD220   Preserved. On USS Intrepid New York from late 1986.
XD221   Crashed in Malaya 6/6/66. Wreck at Sembawang.
XD222   Crashed on 16/11/60, 6 miles north of Blair Gowrie. Ex 736 Sqn.
XD223   Crashed at Changi 20/9/65. Wreck to Foulness. Ex 803 Sqn.
XD224   To Foulness from Aircraft and Armament Experimental Establishment
        February 1970.
XD225   To Larkhill from Fleetlands 1969, Ex Airwork FRU.
XD226   To Arbroath as instructional airframe 1965.
XD227   To Farnborough as apprentice trainer 1969. Thence Larkhill.
XD228   To Royal Aircraft Establishment Bedford in 1967. Ex 736 Sqn.
XD229   To West Freugh. Struck off charge 10/10/66. Ex RAE.
XD230   Crashed in sea off Lossiemouth 28/9/64. Ex 803 Sqn.
XD231   To Farnborough 25/7/69 then scrapped. Ex 800B.
XD232   To Farnborough 5/12/69 then scrapped. Ex FRU.
XD233   No records.
XD234   To Southend thence to Foulness Jan 1971. Ex FRU.
XD235   To Airborne Weapons Research Establishment Foulness March 1970.
        Ex FRU.
XD236   Crashed St. Catherine's Down, IOW, 26/6/68. Ex FRU.
XD237   Crashed at Stripeside Grange Farm, Banffshire 22/2/61. Ex 736 Sqn.

XD238　Crashed at Lossiemouth 6/2/60. Ex 803 Sqn.

XD239　Crashed in Aden Harbour 22/5/63. Ex 800 Sqn.

XD240　Ditched over the side of VICTORIOUS 25/9/58.

XD241　To AWRE Foulness Dec 1970. Ex FRU.

XD242　Written off after belly landing June 1960. Ex 803 Sqn.

XD243　From Lee on Solent to Foulness Sept 1970. Ex 803 Sqn.

XD244　To AWRE Foulness Feb 1971. Ex FRU.

XD245　Crashed into sea 7/2/60. Ex 803 Sqn.

XD246　To AWRE Foulness thence Larkhill, late 1960's.

XD247　Crashed on Black Isle, Ross and Cromarty 19/11/58. Ex 807 Sqn.

XD248　Scrapped at RNAS Brawdy in 1970. Ex FRU.

XD249　Crashed in Firth of Tay 15/11/62. Ex 736 Sqn.

XD250　Crashed in Indian Ocean 17/2/66. Ex 803 Sqn.

XD264　Crashed near Cullen, Morayshire 21/7/61. Ex 803 Sqn.

XD265　Crashed at Milltown during Mirror Airfield Dummy Deck Landing 23/11/62. Ex 736 Sqn.

XD266　Ditched over side of VICTORIOUS 19/11/59. Ex 803 Sqn.

XD267　To RAE Farnborough 16/10/69 to be scrapped. Ex FRU.

XD268　Crashed near Duffus 15/7/65. Ex 800B Sqn.

XD269　Ditched over side of VICTORIOUS 10/7/61. Ex 803 Sqn.

XD270　Crashed in Far East 30/4/65. Ex 800B Sqn.

XD271　To Admiralty Surface Weapons Establishment Foulness from Lee on Solent Sept 1970. Ex 800B.

XD272　To Arbroath as instructional airframe April 1967. Ex 800B.

XD273　Crashed in sea off Borneo 28/4/61. Ex 803 Sqn.

XD274　To Arbroath as instructional airframe 13/10/66. Ex 803 Sqn.

XD275　From Lee on Solent to ASWE Foulness Sept 1970. Ex 800B.

XD276　From Lee on Solent to ASWE Foulness Sept 1970. Ex 803 Sqn.

XD277　Crashed on approach to Changi 6/4/66. Ex 803 Sqn.

XD278　To Arbroath as instructional airframe 4/11/66. Ex 803 Sqn.

XD279　Deck accident ARK ROYAL 2/1/66. Written off. Ex 803.

XD280　To Arbroath as instructional airframe 1/10/66. Ex 800B.

XD281　Crashed at Aberfoyle, Perthshire 10/11/59. Ex 807 Sqn.

XD282　Crashed in Moray Firth 28/1/64. Ex 736 Sqn.

XD316　Crashed in South China Sea 28/1/66. Ex 803 Sqn.

XD317　Preserved in Fleet Air Arm Museum Collection. Ex FRU.

XD318　Crashed in Far East 31/12/65. Ex 803 Sqn.

XD319　Crashed into sea after bolting 7/3/62. Ex 807 Sqn.

XD320　To Naval Aircraft Support Unit, RNAS Brawdy July 1967, Scrapped 1970. Ex 803 Sqn.

XD321　To Naval Aircraft Support Unit, RNAS Brawdy July 1967. Scrapped 1970. Ex 800B.

XD322　To AWRE Foulness 2/12/70. Ex FRU.

XD323　Nosewheel collapsed 18/4/66. Written off. Ex 803 Sqn.

XD324　To Lee on Solent as instructional airframe 14/10/66. Ex 803 Sqn.

XD325   Barrier Landing 7/3/66. Aircraft written off. Ex 803 Sqn.
XD326   Crashed into sea astern of ARK ROYAL 31/7/63. Ex 800 Sqn.
XD327   To Fleetlands 4/9/68 to be scrapped. Ex FRU.
XD328   Barrier landing 3/9/65 thence Fleetlands, scrapped. Ex 803.
XD329   Crashed into sea off Aden 9/12/60. Ex 803 Sqn.
XD330   Scrapped at RNAS Brawdy 1970. Ex 803 Sqn.
XD331   Crashed into sea off HERMES 13/8/62. Ex 803 Sqn.
XD332   Preserved at Helston Aero Park. Ex 764B Sqn.
XD333   To AWRE Foulness Jan 1971. Ex FRU.

Of 76 Scimitars built, 39 were lost in a variety of flying accidents.

736 Squadron Scimitars in line ahead formation, 1962.

SCIMITAR FAMILY ALBUM

The officers of 700 X Squadron. It is the men of this unit who provided the essential link between Development and Squadron service, a vital part of the test process.

A familiar service scene, 800 B Squadron commissioning ceremony. Typical of a time honoured process, the start of so many great things.

1 March 1960. The officers of 804 Squadron on commissioning day with Admiral Sir Martin Dunbar-Naismith, VC.

807 Squadron on commissioning day, 1 October 1958.
Fairey Fulmar (behind) now in FAA Museum.

800 B were adopted by Whitbread Breweries and took the name 'The Foaming Tankards', an allusion to their flight refuelling rôle. Here the CO, Lt. R. Dimmock is seen receiving a ceremonial first draw from the beer dispenser presented to the Squadron by Whitbread.

Top left:
The pilots of 736 Squadron, SBAC show display team in 1962. Left to right: Lt. Cdr. P. Newman (CO), Lt. P. Anderson, Lt. Cdr. J. Kennet, Lt. P. De Souza, Lt. E. Edwards.

Bottom left:
The 807 Squadron display team at Farnborough, 1959. Left to right: Lt. P.J. Lovick, Lt. G.B. Hoddinott, Lt. Cdr. K.A. Leppard. (CO), Lt. P.H. Pearks, Sub. Lt. I.M.B. Aitchison, Lt. D. Pentreath, Lt. Cdr. T.C.S. Leece.

*Typical of many personal service snapshots. P.N. Ewer poses astride his cab
XD322/106 of 800 Squadron, providing a striking head-on view of the aircraft
folded, braced, blanked and tethered.*

SCIMITAR SQUADRON COMMANDERS

700X Squadron
Lt Cdr T G Innes, AFC, RN — 27 August 1957

736 Squadron — June 1959–March 1965
Lt Cdr J D Baker, RN — 2 September 1958
Lt Cdr A Mancais, RN — 2 May 1960
Lt Cdr P G Newman, RN — 9 October 1961
Lt Cdr J A D Ford, RN — 10 January 1963
Lt Cdr J Worth, RN — 9 December 1963

764B Squadron — March 1965–November 1965
Lt Cdr J Worth, RN — 29 March 1965

800 Squadron — July 1959–February 1964
Lt Cdr D P Norman, AFC, RN — 1 July 1959
Lt Cdr A Mancais, RN — 2 October 1961
Lt Cdr D F Mills, RN — 17 December 1962
Lt Cdr P G Newman, RN — 5 March 1962

800B Squadron — September 1964–August 1966
Lt R Dimmock, RN — 9 September 1964
Lt Cdr N Grier-Rees, RN — 20 October 1965

803 Squadron — June 1958–October 1966
Cdr J D Russell, RN — 3 June 1958
Lt Cdr G R Higgs, RN — 25 September 1958
Lt Cdr A J Leahy, MBE, DSC, RN — 14 December 1959
Lt Cdr T C S Leece, RN — 18 December 1960
Lt Cdr N J P Mills, RN — 1 August 1962
Lt Cdr P G Newman, RN — 4 May 1964
Lt Cdr J Worth, RN — 14 June 1965

804 Squadron — March 1960–September 1961
Lt Cdr T V G Binney, RN — 1 March 1960

807 Squadron — October 1958–May 1962
Lt Cdr K A Leppard, RN — 1 October 1958
Lt Cdr W A Tofts, RN — 19 September 1959
Lt Cdr G A Rowan-Thompson, RN — 1 March 1961

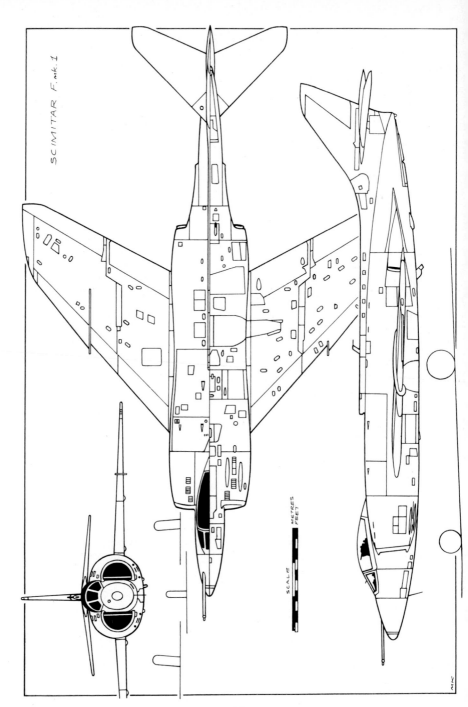

SCIMITAR F.mk.1

SCALE

METRES
FEET

44

LEADING PARTICULARS

DIMENSIONS

Span	37′ 2″ (11.3 m)
Span folded	20′ 6½″ (6.16 m)
Length	55′ 3″ (16.25 m)
Height	17′ 4″ (5.28 m)
Gross wing area	484.9 sq ft (45.05 sq m)
Sweepback	45° at 25° chord.

WEIGHTS

Fuel	1,064 gallons (4,837 litres) internal
	200 gallons (3,636.8 litres) in four drop tanks
Empty weight	23962 lb (10,869 kg)
All up weight	34200 lb (15,513 kg)

POWERPLANT

Two Rolls-Royce Avon RA 24 or RA 28 CF 10,000 lb static thrust. Later Avon 200 series.

PERFORMANCE

Maximum speed 640 kts (1,186kph)
Mach 0.968 at sea level.
587 kts (1,088 kph) at 20,000 ft (9.144 m)
Normal range 1,422 miles (2,288 km) at 35,000 ft
Time to 5000 ft (1,524 m) 1.3 min.
Time to 45,000 ft (13,216 m) 6.65 min
Service ceiling 46,000 ft (14020 m).

STORES

4 x 30 mm Aden cannons
4 x 1000 lb Bombs
4 x Bullpup air to ground missiles
4 x Sidewinder air to air missiles
2′ & 3″ rocket projectiles or other alternatives
including 4 x 200 gallon drop tanks.

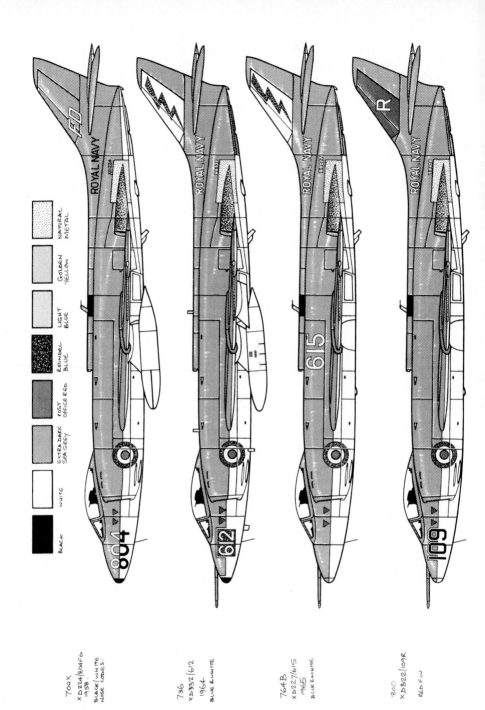

ROYAL NAVY

700X
XD224/804FD
1958.
BLACK/WHITE
NOSE CONES.

736
XD332/612
1964
BLUE & WHITE

764B
XD227/615
1965
BLUE & WHITE

800
XD322/109R
RED FIN

NATURAL
METAL

GOLDEN
YELLOW

LIGHT
BLUE

ROUNDEL
BLUE

POST
OFFICE RED

EXTRA DARK
SEA GREY

WHITE

BLACK

46

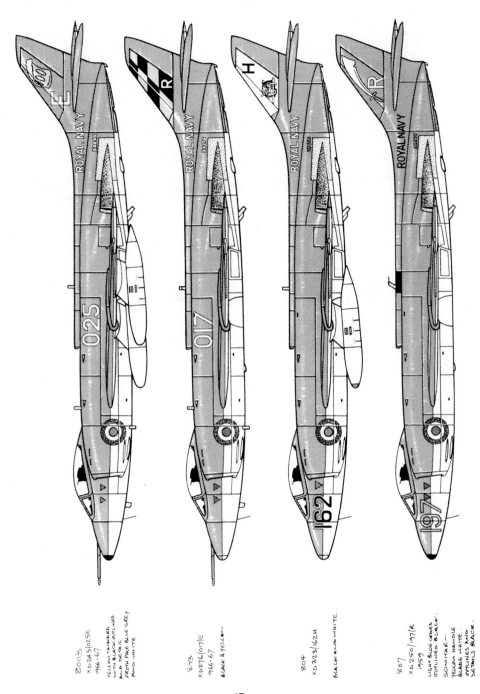

800B
XD243/025E
1966-67
YELLOW TAILGUARD
WITH BLACK OUTLINES
AND DETAIL.
FROM PALE BLUE-GREY
AND WHITE.

803
XD276/017/E
1966-67
BLACK & YELLOW

804
XD323/162H
BLACK AND WHITE.

807
XD250/197/R
1959
LIGHT BLUE COMES
OUTLINED BLACK.

SCIMITAR—
YELLOW HANDLE
BLADE WHITE
OUTLINES AND
DETAILS BLACK.

47

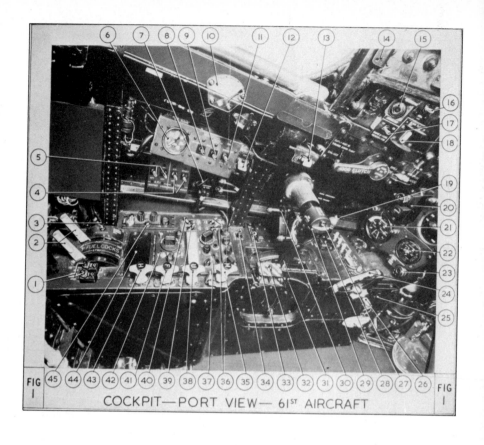

COCKPIT—PORT VIEW— 61ST AIRCRAFT

FIG
I

FIG
I

48

Key to Fig. 1

1. Engine ignition circuit breakers (two)
2. L.P. fuel cocks (two)
3. External intercomm. switch
4. Blue Silk control switches (two)
5. G.P.I. control switches (two)
6. Emergency System hydraulic pressure gauge
7. Windscreen de-icing cock
8. V.P. azimuth elevation switch
9. V.P. meter sensitivity switch
10. Hood rails locked indicator
11. Standby U.H.F. emergency P to Tx switch
12. IFF, ARN 21–EP, EL fusing inverter switch
13. High intensity light switch
14. Position for LABS controller
15. Telebriefing connected light
16. Telebriefing call switch
17. Radar ranging presentation switch
18. Blown flaps switch
19. Target reject switch
20. Undercarriage pushbuttons (two)
21. Wheelbrakes triple pressure gauge
22. Undercarriage position indicator
23. Hook down light
24. Hood jettison handle
25. Hood jettison handle safety pin stowage
26. Hood jettison handle safety pin
27. P to T pushbutton
28. Engine starting pushbuttons (two)
29. Airbrakes switch
30. Engine relight pushbuttons (two)
31. Throttles friction lever
32. Duplicate trim switch
33. Autostabiliser switch
34. Rudder trim switch
35. Emergency hydraulic system master control handle
36. U.H.F. set selector and standby power switches (two)
37. Radio controller
38. Undercarriage emergency handle
39. Standby U.H.F. channel selector
40. Radio altimeter switch
41. Flaps emergency handle
42. I.F.F. controller
43. Hook emergency handle
44. Position for S.I.F. controller
45. Tacan controller

49

FIG
2

FIG
2

COCKPIT— FRONT VIEW— 61ˢᵀ AIRCRAFT

50

46. Voltmeter and alternative position
47. Radio altimeter height band selector
48. Hood clutch lever
49. G.P.I. variation setting control
50. Airbrakes magnetic indicator
51. Flaps selector lever
52. Hood selector lever
53. Flap override switch
54. Cockpit emergency lights switch
55. Arrester hook selector switch
56. External stores jettison switch
57. Port 'attention getter' light
58. Accelerometer
59. Feel simulator one failed magnetic indicator
60. Radio altimeter limit lights (three)
61. Parking brake handle
62. Gun sight
63. Oxygen flow magnetic indicator
64. Tacan indicator
65. Air to air refuelling master switch
66. Oil pressure magnetic indicators (two)
67. Green Salad or Violet Picture indicator
68. Starboard 'attention getter' light
69. Drop tank fuel transfer indicator
70. Engine r.p.m. indicators (two)
71. Summation fuel contents gauge
72. J.p.t. indicators (two)
73. Artificial horizon standby power switch
74. High intensity light
75. Fuel contents gauges (eight)
76. Booster pump failure warning lights (eight)
77. Fuel pressure magnetic indicators (two)
78. Cockpit altimeter
79. Oxygen contents gauge
80. Fuel balancing retrim switch
81. Booster pump failure selector switch
82. De-icing magnetic indicator
83. Guard for 'all armament' trigger switch
84. Tailplane and aileron trim switch
85. Camera switch
86. Valve 'B' failure switch
87. Fuel flowmeter
88. No. 1 inverter fail magnetic indicator
89. Flight instrument reset switch
90. Drop tanks selector switch
91. J.p.t. control switches (two)
92. Nos. 1 and 2 systems hydraulic pressure gauges (two)
93. Drop tanks fuel override switch
94. Take-off safe trim magnetic indicators (two)
95. Radio altimeter indicator
96. Fuselage flaps indicator
97. 'Blown flaps on' light
98. Trailing edge flaps position indicator
99. Tailplane position indicator
100. Leading edge flaps locked magnetic indicator
101. Battery isolation switch
102. Fuel master switch
103. Pressure head heater switch
104. Engine selection switches (two)
105. Instrument early start switch

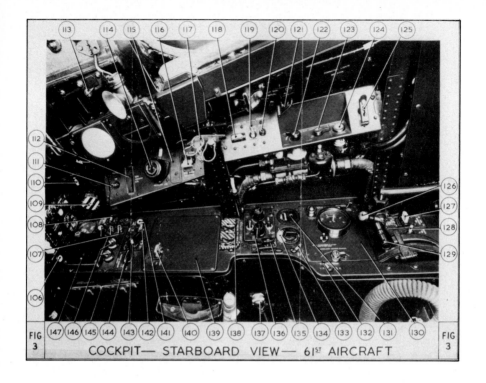

COCKPIT— STARBOARD VIEW — 61ST AIRCRAFT

FIG 3

52

106. Recuperator failure magnetic indicator
107. Standard warning panel switches (three)
108. Firebell normal/off switch
109. Cockpit manual vent
110. G.G.S. Practice switch
111. Cockpit lights master switch
112. Cockpit general lights dimmer switch
113. Starboard louvre
114. Ancillary lights off/dimmer switch
115. Position for target towing master switch
116. Gunsight dive bomb selector switch
117. Stowage for sear pins
118. Navigation lights switch
119. Navigation lights bright/dim switch
120. Formation lights switch
121. Hood seal manual inflation cock
122. Ventilated suit temperature control
123. Ventilated suit flow control
124. Wing-and-nose locked magnetic indicator
125. Carrier/airfield switch
126. Anti-G on/off cock
127. Ice detector test switch
128. Fire detection test switch
129. Wingfold control lever
130. Oxygen regulator
131. Flowmeter specific gravity compensator
132. Windscreen demisting switch
133. Cabin air master switch
134. Cabin air temperature control
135. Ice detection and engine anti-icing switch
136. G.G.S. controller
137. Emergency oxygen handle
138. Stores jettison pylon switches (three)
139. Detachable panel for change of role
140. R.P. switch
141. Radar failure magnetic indicator
142. Radar on/off switch
143. R.P. selector switch
144. Master armament selector switch
145. Stowage for ejection seat main and secondary firing handles safety pins (two)
146. Fire-extinguisher pushbuttons (two)
147. Standard warning panel.